CLIFTON PARK-HALFMOON PUBLIC LIBRARY

W9-AMP-316

A Note to Parents and Teachers

Kids can imagine, kids can laugh and kids can learn to read with this exciting new series of first readers. Each book in the Kids Can Read series has been especially written, illustrated and designed for beginning readers. Humorous, easy-to-read stories, appealing characters and topics, and engaging illustrations make for books that kids will want to read over and over again.

To make selecting a book easy for kids, parents and teachers, the Kids Can Read series offers three levels based on different reading abilities:

Level 1: Kids Can Start to Read

Short stories, simple sentences, easy vocabulary, lots of repetition and visual clues for kids just beginning to read.

Level 2: Kids Can Read with Help

Longer stories, varied sentences, increased vocabulary, some repetition and visual clues for kids who have some reading skills, but may need a little help.

Level 3: Kids Can Read Alone

More challenging topics, more complex sentences, advanced vocabulary, language play, minimal repetition and visual clues for kids who are reading by themselves.

With the Kids Can Read series, kids can enter a new and exciting world of reading!

How Animals Eat

Written by **Pamela Hickman**
Illustrated by **Pat Stephens**

Kids Can Press

Clifton Park - Halfmoon Public Library
475 Moe Road
Clifton Park, New York 12065

To Caitlin — P.S.

 ® Kids Can Read is a registered trademark of Kids Can Press Ltd.

Text © 2001 Pamela Hickman
Illustrations © 2001 Pat Stephens
Revised edition © 2007

All rights reserved. No part of this publication may be reproduced, stored in a
retrieval system or transmitted, in any form or by any means, without the prior
written permission of Kids Can Press Ltd. or, in case of photocopying or othe
reprographic copying, a license from The Canadian Copyright Licensing Agency
(Access Copyright). For an Access Copyright license, visit www.accesscopyright.ca
or call toll free to 1-800-893-5777.

Kids Can Press acknowledges the financial support of the Government of Ontario,
through the Ontario Media Development Corporation's Ontario Book Initiative; the
Ontario Arts Council; the Canada Council for the Arts; and the Government of Canada,
through the BPIDP, for our publishing activity.

Published in Canada by
Kids Can Press Ltd.
29 Birch Avenue
Toronto, ON M4V 1E2

Published in the U.S. by
Kids Can Press Ltd.
2250 Military Road
Tonawanda, NY 14150

www.kidscanpress.com

Adapted by David MacDonald from the book *Animals Eating*.

Edited by David MacDonald
Designed by Sherill Chapman
Educational consultant: Maureen Skinner Weiner, United Synagogue Day School,
Willowdale, Ontario

Printed and bound in Singapore

The hardcover edition of this book is smyth sewn casebound.
The paperback edition of this book is limp sewn with a drawn-on cover.

CM 07 0 9 8 7 6 5 4 3 2 1
CM PA 07 0 9 8 7 6 5 4 3 2 1

Library and Archives Canada Cataloguing in Publication

Hickman, Pamela
   How animals eat / written by Pamela Hickman ; illustrated by Pat Stephens.

(Kids Can read)
Based on author's Animals eating.

ISBN-13: 978-1-55453-031-1 (bound) ISBN-10: 1-55453-031-8 (bound)
ISBN-13: 978-1-55453-032-8 (pbk.) ISBN-10: 1-55453-032-6 (pbk.)

1. Animals — Food — Juvenile literature. I. Stephens, Pat, 1950– II. Title.
III. Series: Kids Can read (Toronto, Ont.)

QL756.5.H52 2007   j591.5'3   C2006-903042-1

0215

Kids Can Press is a *fOrUs*™ Entertainment company

Contents

Time to eat!

What would it be like to catch your food with your tongue? A chameleon knows. Do you carry stones in your stomach to help grind up your food? That's what a crocodile does.

Get ready to meet some amazing animals and find out how they eat and drink.

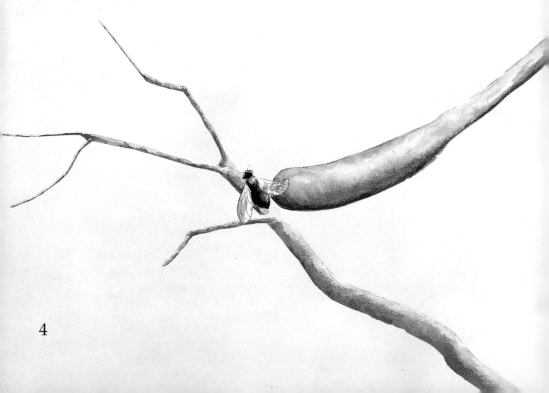

Chameleon

Food from nature

Nature has something for every animal to eat. A mouse may nibble on some seeds. A snake may swallow the mouse. And an owl may catch the snake.

Dormouse

Some animals eat plants and some animals eat meat. Other animals eat plants and meat.

Who eats what?

Can you guess what each of these animals eats? Turn to page 32 for the answers.

Many mouths

Mouths come in many shapes and sizes. Most animals have a mouth that is just right for the kind of food they eat.

Some animals have extra-long tongues for catching insects. Meat eaters have sharp teeth for killing and tearing up food.

If you were a crocodile …

- you would have large, strong jaws and sharp teeth for grabbing animals you want to eat. Then you would drag your meal underwater.
- you would carry stones in your stomach to help grind up your food.
- you would eat fish and some other animals — including people!

Crocodile

9

Stick out your tongue

Take another look at the chameleon's tongue on pages 4–5. This amazing tongue can catch and pull in an insect faster than you can blink!

A hairy woodpecker can stick its long tongue down insect tunnels to catch ants and beetles.

Hairy woodpecker

A toad's tongue is attached to the front of its mouth. (Your tongue is attached at the back.) A sticky pad on the end of its tongue helps the toad catch bugs.

Toad

The anteater has a tongue that is shaped like a worm. This long, sticky tongue is perfect for catching thousands of ants and termites every day. The giant anteater's tongue is longer than your arm!

Anteater

Pass the plants, please

Different animals may eat from the same
plant. A rabbit may nibble the leaves of a
plant. An insect may feed on the plant's
roots. A hummingbird may lap
up nectar from the plant's
flower. A mouse may feed on the
plant's seeds.

Now look up, way up,
to find out what is
special about
the giraffe.

Giraffe

If you were a giraffe ...

- you would be the tallest animal on Earth.
- your long legs and neck would help you reach food that other animals could not get to.
- you would wrap your tongue around leaves and pull them into your mouth.
- your tongue would have a natural sunscreen to protect it from the hot sun.

Snacking on seeds

All plants with flowers make seeds. The seeds are food for many hungry animals.

A blue jay traps a large seed under its toes. Then it uses its beak to hammer at the seed until it breaks open.

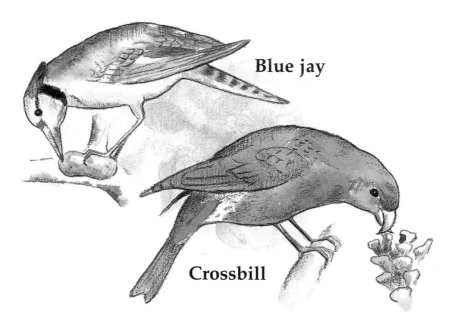

Blue jay

Crossbill

The crossbill has a sharp, curved beak. This kind of beak is perfect for getting the seeds out of cones.

Cheeky

The European hamster has cheeks that are like big pockets. These pockets are great for collecting seeds. The hamster carries the seeds back to its home to save them for a winter snack.

If the hamster is attacked, it will blow the seeds into the face of its enemy. This gives the hamster time to escape.

Using your nose

The bison is the largest land animal in North America. It eats grass all year round.

So what does the bison do in winter when all the grass is covered with snow? It uses its large, flat nose as a snowplow to uncover the grass.

Picky eaters

Some animals can eat only one kind of food.

The giant panda eats only
the soft leaves and
stems of the bamboo
plant. And it eats
a lot of them!
A giant panda
feeds for 10 to 12
hours a day.

Giant panda

Meat on the menu

Animals that eat meat spend most of their days trying to find and kill their next meal. Many meat eaters have good eyes, ears and noses to help them hunt.

Some animals, such as the mink, hunt alone. Other animals, such as the wolf, go hunting in groups.

Longtail weasel

If you were a longtail weasel …

- your strong jaws and sharp teeth would help you kill and hold on to animals such as mice, squirrels, birds and rabbits.
- inside the burrow where you live, you would store food for the winter.
- if you live where it snows, your brown coat would turn white in winter. This would help you hide while you hunt.

Open wide!

Snakes have special jaws that can open very, very wide. A snake can swallow a whole animal, even one that is bigger than its head!

Python eating a deer

A python is one of the largest snakes in the world. It hunts by wrapping its strong body around an animal and squeezing it until it dies. The python then swallows the animal whole.

Fast food

After a snake eats a huge meal, it doesn't need to eat again for a long time. Other animals need to eat all the time to get the energy they need.

Hummingbirds use up a lot of energy every day. They must eat all the time to stay alive.

Hummingbird

Waste not, want not

In nature, animals that eat the leftovers of another animal's meal are called scavengers. They wait for another animal to make a kill, then they move in to eat up whatever is left. Turkey vultures are expert scavengers.

Turkey vulture

If you were a turkey vulture ...

- you would feed mainly on dead animals.
- you would have good eyesight and an excellent sense of smell to help you find food.
- you would use your long, hooked beak and sharp claws to tear the flesh off dead animals.

Get in line

When you sit down to a meal, your family shares the food on your table. Wild animals that live together in families, such as wolves or lions, also share their food.

In wolf families, the head male and female wolves eat first. The rest of the wolves join in later.

Wolves

Saving snacks

Some animals save food when there is lots of it. They keep it for times when food is hard to find. Here are some animals and the food they save.

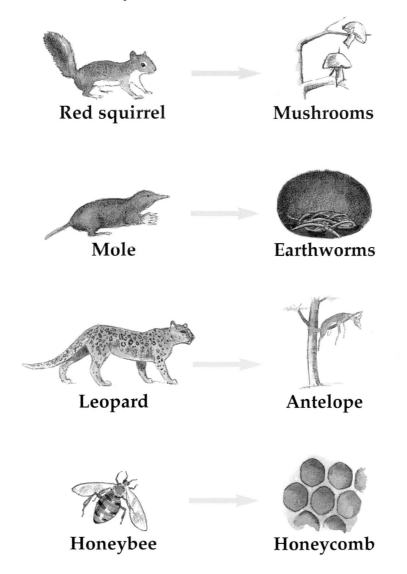

Red squirrel → Mushrooms

Mole → Earthworms

Leopard → Antelope

Honeybee → Honeycomb

Feeling thirsty?

All living things need water. When you feel thirsty, your body is telling you that it needs more water.

Animals get the water they need in different ways. Many animals drink through their mouth just like you do.

Lion

Animals drinking at a watering hole in Africa

Zebras

Giraffes

Jackals

Frogs and toads don't drink through their mouths. They soak up the water they need through their skin.

Koalas don't drink because they get all the water they need in the leaves they eat.

Koala

Living on liquids

For some animals, drinking is not just a way of getting water. It is also how they get their food.

Vampire bats are famous for getting their food by drinking blood. This lamprey feeds on the blood of other fish.

Lamprey

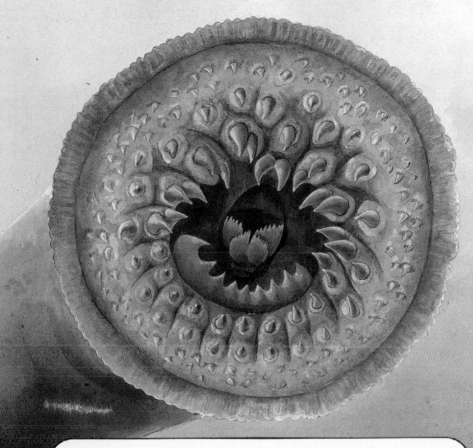

If you were a lamprey ...

- you wouldn't have any jaws. You would have a round, sucking mouth that could attach itself to another fish.
- your mouth would have as many as 125 sharp teeth. You would move these teeth back and forth to drill a hole into a fish's body and then drink its blood.

Something sweet

For hummingbirds and some bats, a flower's nectar is a sweet treat. These animals have long tongues to help them reach down inside a flower to lap up its nectar. Some insects also feed on nectar.

Long-nosed bat

Hummingbird

Sapsuckers like to feed on tree sap. They use their hard, pointed beaks to make holes in tree trunks. The holes fill with sweet sap, and the birds lick it up with their long tongues.

Sapsucker

Answers

Here is what the animals on page 7 eat.

- Bee flies and male mosquitos feed on flowers.

- Female mosquitos feed on blood from animals such as birds and moose, as well as human blood.

- Moose eat plants.

- Dragonflies eat mosquitos.

- Frogs eat insects.

- Herons eat frogs and fish.

- Fish eat frogs and insects.

- Ospreys eat fish.

MAY   2007

CLIFTON PARK-HALFMOON PUBLIC LIBRARY

0 00 06 0294021 5